CHINA

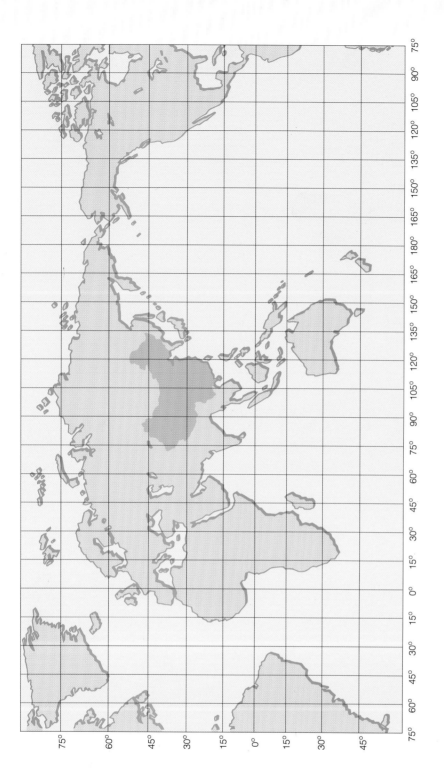

In addition to China's 22 provinces, there are:

5 AUTONOMOUS REGIONS

NEI MONGGOL (Inner Mongolia)
XIZANG (Tibet)
XINJIANG UYGUR
GUANGXI
NINGXIA

3 MUNICIPALITIES

BEIJING
TIANJIN
SHANGHAI

COUNTRY
FACT FILES

CHINA

Catherine Charley

RAINTREE STECK-VAUGHN
PUBLISHERS

Austin, Texas

Design Roger Kohn
Editor Diana Russell, Helene Resky
DTP editor Helen Swansbourne
Picture research Valerie Mulcahy
Illustration János Márffy
Calligraphy Leon Leung
Consultant Ruth Cherrington
Commissioning editor Debbie Fox

We are grateful to the following for permission
to reproduce photographs:
Front Cover: Tony Stone Images *above*, Spectrum Colour
Library (D. & J. Heaton) *below;* Aspect Picture Library, pages 9
(Peter Carmichael), 13 *below* (Ma Po Shum); Cephas Picture
Library/Nigel Blythe, pages 13 *above*, 22 *above*, 26 *below*, 34
above; Catherine Charley, page 21 *above* and *below*; China
National Tourist Office, page 8; Colorific!, pages 24 (Steve
Benbow), 34 *below* (Cary Wolinsky); Eye Ubiquitous/TRIP,
page 12; Sally and Richard Greenhill, page 23; Robert Harding
Picture Library, pages 20 and 25 (G. & P. Corrigan), 26–27, 29
(Peter Scholey), 32, 39 *above* (Gavin Hellier), 39 *below*; The
Image Bank/Chinese Photo Association, page 17; Magnum,
pages 18 *above* (Patrick Zachmann), 27 *below,* 33 and 38
below (Hiroji Kubota), 38 *above* (Michael K. Nichols), 40
(Bruno Barbey): Spectrum Colour Library, pages 35, 37
(D. & J. Heaton); Frank Spooner Pictures/Alistair Berg, page
36 *below*; Frank Spooner Pictures/Gamma, pages 14 (Remi
Benali), 18 *below,* and 36 *above* (Anderson), 30 (Chip Hires);
Tony Stone Images, pages 22 *below* (Alain le Garsmeur), 31
(Julian Calder), 41, 43 (John Callahan); Sygma, pages 15 and
42 (Kees), 28 (G. Rancinan), TRIP/Keith Cardwell, page 10
above; WWF Photolibrary, page 16 (Mauri Rautkari); Zefa,
page 10 *below*.

Special thanks to Laura Rivkin and all the staff at the
Great Britain–China Centre, London

The statistics given in this book are the most up-to-date
available at the time of going to press

Printed and bound in Hong Kong by Paramount Printing Group

1 2 3 4 5 6 7 8 9 0 HK 99 98 97 96 95 94

Library of Congress Cataloging-in-Publication Data
Charley, Catherine.
China / Catherine Charley.
p. cm. – (Country fact files)
Includes bibliographical references and index.
ISBN 0-8114-2789-7
1. China – Juvenile literature. [1. China.]
I. Title. II. Series.
DS706.C4762 1995
951–dc20
94-15613
CIP AC

**C
O
N
T
E
N
T
S**

Words that are explained in the glossary are printed in
SMALL CAPITALS the first time they are mentioned in the text.

The only human-made object on Earth that can be seen from the moon is the Great Wall of China. The wall stretches for 4,600 miles (7,400 km) across the north of China. China is the third largest country in the world (after Canada and the Russian Federation), and nearly a quarter of the world's population lives there. It is a country that has a long history, but it is also changing fast.

The Chinese word for China is *Zhongguo*, which means "Middle Country." The ancient Chinese felt themselves to be the center of the world. They had a highly developed civilization, and for hundreds of years they traded silk and other goods with countries in Central Asia and Europe.

As Europe began to modernize in the 15th century, China was trying to preserve its old traditions, and so its emperors closed the country to outsiders. In the 19th century, as China suffered from weak government and natural disasters like famines, Western nations took control of parts of the territory.

In the early 20th century the COMMUNIST Party, established in 1921 and led by Mao Zedong, won the support of many of the Chinese people, especially in the countryside. In 1949, after a long civil war, the Communists defeated the Nationalist Party, led by Chiang Kai-Shek, and the People's Republic of China (PRC) was founded. For many years contact with CAPITALIST nations was discouraged. However, in the early 1980s, the government introduced the "Reform and Open Door Policy," which relaxed controls over industry and trade and allowed more contact with other countries.

These reforms are now affecting all areas of people's lives. They are raising the standard of living but are also one of the major reasons for growing problems, such as inflation, corruption, and overcrowding in cities. The 1990s are a challenging time for the Chinese people.

◄ *Pan Pan the panda, the emblem of the Pan Asian Games held in Beijing in 1990. Holding the games there was a sign to the world that China is no longer isolated.*

► *China now has many FREE MARKETS, where people do not have to buy and sell goods at prices set by the government. But this approach conflicts with strict Communist ideals.*

● Area: 3,696,032 square miles (9,572,678 sq km) excluding Taiwan and Hong Kong
● Population (1993): 1.2 billion
● Population density: 320 persons per square mile (124 per sq km)
● Capital: Beijing, population 7.5 million
● Other main cities: Shanghai 8.3 million; Tianjin 7 million; Shenyang 4.2 million; Wuhan 3.4 million; Guangzhou 3.4 million; Chongqing 2.8 million; Harbin 2.8 million; Chengdu 2.6 million; Xi'an 2.5 million; Nanjing 2.5 million; Zibo 2.5 million; Dalian 2.4 million; Jinan 2.3 million; Changchun 2.1 million; Qingdao 2 million
(24 other cities have a population over 1 million)
● Highest mountain: Mount Everest (Qomolangma) 29,028 feet (8,848 m)

● Longest river: Yangtze (Chang Jiang) 3,237 miles (5,470 km)
● Official language: Mandarin Chinese
● Major religions: BUDDHISM, DAOISM, Confucianism, Islam, Christianity, Judaism
● Currency: Renminbi, written as RMB. Units: 1 Yuan = 10 Jiao = 100 Fen
● Economy: Agriculturally based. Most urban areas are highly industrialized.
● Major resources: Large rivers, coal, iron ore, oil, gas, tin, tungsten, aluminum, other minerals
● Major products: Bicycles, paper, textiles, silk products, wheat, rice, tea, soybeans
● Environmental problems: Deforestation; grasslands turning into deserts; pollution of air, water, and land near industrial areas and in cities

THE LANDSCAPE

China covers almost 3.7 million square miles (9.6 million sq km). The landscape descends like a staircase from the high mountain ranges of the west (the highest is the Himalayas), across the Tibet/Qinghai plateau and the lower mountain ranges and plains of eastern China, to the Pacific coast. Most of the mountain ranges run from west to east. The main rivers flow west to east, or north to south. Many of the ranges in the west are shared by countries bordering China, such as India, Nepal, Pakistan, and Russia.

▲*The limestone hills and mountains in Guilin in southern China are famous for their unusual shape.*

▼*The Himalayas in the southwest of Tibet are the highest mountains in the world. Every available piece of arable land in China is cultivated, even at this altitude.*

KEY FACTS

- China's lowest point is the Turpan Basin in the north-west: 503 feet (154 m) below sea level.
- Almost 26 percent of China lies above 10,000 feet (3,000 m).
- China has nearly 11,000 miles (18,000 km) of coastline.
- China covers one-fifth of Asia.
- There is just one time zone in China. It runs on Beijing time, so it can be light at midnight in Xinjiang region in the west.

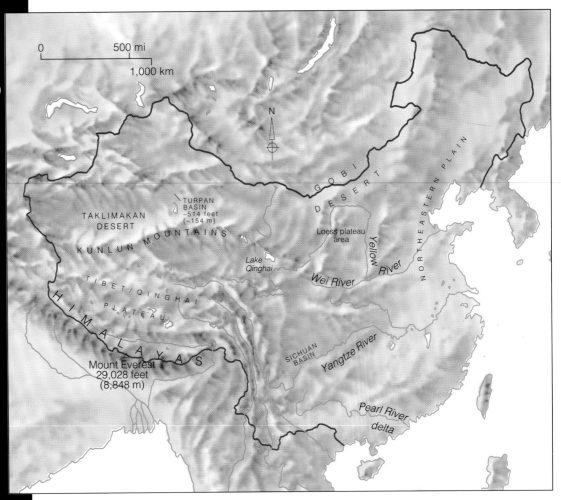

The Tibet/Qinghai plateau, often called the "Roof of the World," is the largest highland region on Earth, with an area of over 772,200 square miles (2 million sq km). It covers 23 percent of China and is situated at an average altitude of 14,800 feet (4,500 m) above sea level. North of this plateau, beyond the Kunlun range, lies Xinjiang Autonomous Region, much of which is desert. Here is the Taklimakan Desert, one of the largest sand deserts in the world, stretching over 115,830 square miles (300,000 sq km). The Gobi Desert extends east from the Taklimakan Desert into Mongolia. It is separated from the Taklimakan by a series of oases.

Northern China's most important natural features are the Yellow River (Huang Ho), named after the color of the sediment it carries along its route, and the LOESS plateau. The river, 2,697 miles (4,345 km) long, flows roughly west to east. It makes a large loop, north and then south, through the fertile loess plateau before entering the Northeastern Plain. One-third of China's

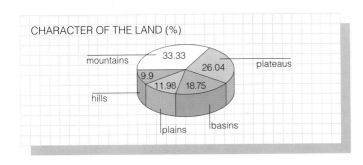

CHARACTER OF THE LAND (%)

mountains 33.33
plateaus 26.04
basins 18.75
plains 11.98
hills 9.9

population lives in this region. Chinese civilization began over 4,000 years ago in the valleys of the Yellow River and the Wei River, which joins it.

At 3,915 miles (6,300 km), the Yangtze (Chang Jiang) is China's longest river and the third longest in the world (after the Nile and Amazon). Chang Jiang means "long river" in Chinese. Its source is west of Lake Qinghai on the Tibet/Qinghai plateau, from where it flows south and then eastward before it reaches the Pacific at Shanghai.

The Yangtze is the official division between north and south China. In some cities that lie on both sides of the river, heating is provided for homes on the north side but not on the south, in spite of the fact that the temperature is the same.

Much of China south of the Yangtze is particularly mountainous. The middle and lower Yangtze plains, and the Pearl River delta (Zhujiangkou) around Guangzhou, are where most of China's rice is grown. The Sichuan Basin is another great rice-growing area. This basin, which is surrounded by mountains, was formed from a huge prehistoric lake that left behind red soil deposits. It lies at an altitude of between 1,000 to 2,330 feet (300 and 700 m).

▼*The Yellow River collects yellow-colored silt as it flows through the loess regions of central and northern China.*

CLIMATE AND WEATHER

▶This gorge and its caves are near the Turpan oasis in the desert region of north-west China.

▼Tropical plants grow on Hainan Island off the coast of southern China. It is sometimes referred to as "China's Hawaii."

The climate and weather in China are varied because of the country's size, landscape, and location. China is so vast that it covers 30° of latitude from north to south and more than 60° of longitude from west to east. Bitterly cold winds from Siberia blow over the north at the same time as tropical plants grow in the south. In winter the temperature can be −4°F (−20°C) in the northeastern city of Harbin near the Russian border, while at the same time it is 68°F (20°C) in Haikou on Hainan Island in the far south.

Because of the varied landscape, even places near each other can have very different temperatures. In summer, the temperature in the northern part of the Tibetan highlands never reaches more than 50°F (10°C), while in the Turpan Basin just 928 miles (1,000 km) farther north, it can be as high as 116°F (47°C).

China's position between the large land-mass of the Asian continent and the Pacific Ocean means the climate is affected by the cycle of the monsoon winds. This is caused by the temperature difference between the land and the ocean. In the winter, bitterly cold dry winds blow from the interior of the continent over west and north China. Sometimes the winds bring dust from the desert and the loess regions. Winter in the south is milder. But there can be spells of cold, wet weather if winds move inland from the ocean.

In the summer, warm moist winds enter

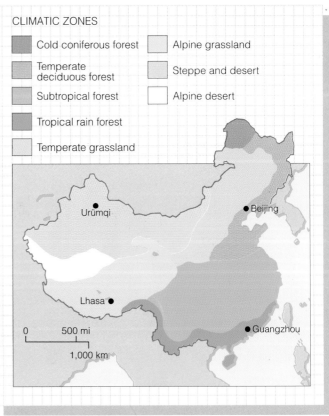

▲The Ice Lantern Festival is held in the northeastern city of Harbin from January to March every year. Buildings and other sculptures are made entirely from ice, and colored lanterns are hung up inside them.

southern China, making it hot and humid and bringing rain. These winds usually carry rain into the rest of China, but the pattern is irregular. If the winds move too quickly toward north China, the central regions can suffer drought, and floods occur in the north. Alternatively, if the winds meet northern air currents, they will drop all their rain in central China, and the northern regions might experience drought.

For centuries the Chinese have been building irrigation systems, canals, dikes, and dams to try and control the water

CLIMATIC ZONES

- Cold coniferous forest
- Temperate deciduous forest
- Subtropical forest
- Tropical rain forest
- Temperate grassland
- Alpine grassland
- Steppe and desert
- Alpine desert

Urŭmqi · Beijing · Lhasa · 0 500 mi 1,000 km Guangzhou ·

KEY FACTS

● On average the temperature drops 9–11°F (5–6°C) for every 3,300 feet (1,000 m) of altitude.

● Kunming, the capital of Yunnan province, is known as "Spring City" because its climate is so good all year round.

● Chongqing, Wuhan, and Nanjing are called "the three furnaces" by the Chinese, because of their long, hot, and humid summers.

● Typhoons are likely to hit the southeast coast between June and September.

▲*Many parts of China often suffer from bad flooding. In the summer of 1991, 200 million people in east central China were affected by widespread and serious floods.*

supply and prevent flooding. However, there are still many natural disasters. The Yellow River is known as "China's sorrow" because of the devastation caused when it floods. Over the centuries the silt carried by the Yellow River has built up, raising the riverbed to a level that is higher than the land alongside it. Dikes have been built, but if the water is high, they do not work. The Yangtze River also floods badly.

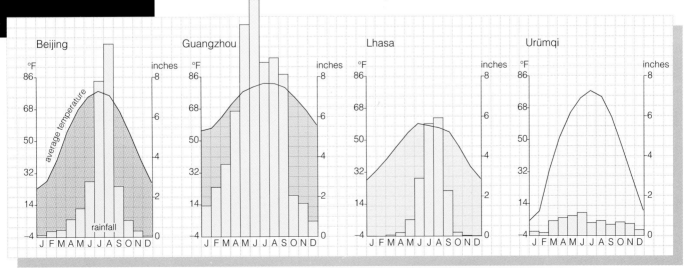

China has a large supply of natural resources. Coal provides 75 percent of its energy. The biggest coal deposits are in the north. Oil and natural gas also provide sources of energy. Many of the oil deposits are in the northwest, and there are offshore oil fields in the East and South China Seas. It is believed that China has large reserves of oil both onshore and offshore, and various projects to explore these are under way, some of which are being carried out with foreign aid.

Most of China's water resources are in remote areas in the south and southwest. Water only provides 5 percent of China's energy, with various hydroelectric projects bringing power to small, local areas. The largest dam is on the Yangtze at Gezhouba in Hubei province. A project to build the world's biggest dam and hydroelectric power station is now in progress in the Three Gorges in the middle section of the

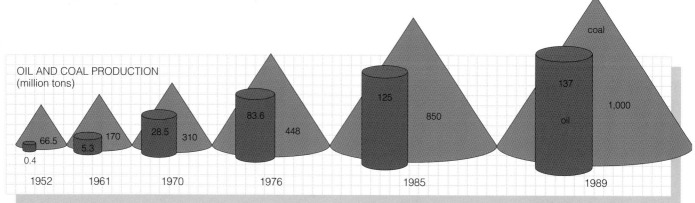

OIL AND COAL PRODUCTION
(million tons)

	1952	1961	1970	1976	1985	1989
oil	0.4	5.3	28.5	83.6	125	137
coal	66.5	170	310	448	850	1,000

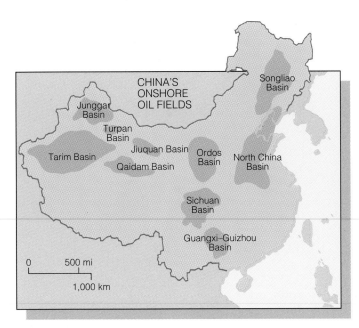

CHINA'S ONSHORE OIL FIELDS

Songliao Basin
Junggar Basin
Turpan Basin
Tarim Basin
Jiuquan Basin
Qaidam Basin
Ordos Basin
North China Basin
Sichuan Basin
Guangxi–Guizhou Basin

0 500 mi
1,000 km

◀ **Coal is loaded onto barges on the Yangtze River at Wanxian in Sichuan province, to be transported to other parts of China.**

▼ **Drilling for oil in the desert of the Xinjiang Autonomous Region in north-west China. China has both onshore and offshore oil reserves.**

Yangtze River. This project is proving to be controversial, as it involves moving one million people from their homes and flooding a large area of natural beauty. There are still enormous forests in the northeast and Tibet, providing timber for the paper industry.

China has abundant iron reserves, though they have a low iron content, and it is the world's principal producer of tungsten, which is used in light bulbs. There are large reserves of manganese and many other metals that are essential for the development of the steel industry. China also has deposits of lead, zinc, mercury, antimony, bauxite, silver, gold, aluminum, uranium, and platinum.

The main problem is finding the best way to exploit the country's natural resources. Most are found in remote regions, far away from the industrial areas of central and eastern China. The hostile landscape means it is difficult and expensive to build transportation links.

KEY FACTS

● China has deposits of most of the world's minerals.
● China is the world's largest coal producer.
● On the grasslands of Inner Mongolia, wind power supplies electricity for electric fences to prevent stock from roaming.
● A nuclear power station opened near Shanghai in 1991. A second one is under construction in Guangdong province.

◈ POPULATION

Today 1.2 billion people live in China, more than in any other country in the world. The population has expanded rapidly since the 1950s. To stop it from rising more steeply, in 1980 the government introduced a policy that limits most couples to having only one child. Despite this, it is estimated that the population will be over 1.3 billion by the beginning of the 21st century.

The one-child policy is controversial because the Chinese traditionally have large families. In the cities most couples have followed the policy, but in the countryside people want more than one child. They particularly want a son to work on the land; keep the family name going; and look after them in their old age. In the countryside, the one-child policy has now been relaxed slightly.

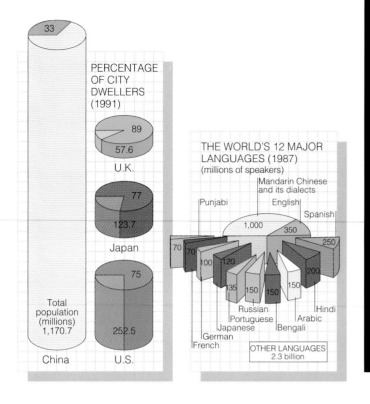

PERCENTAGE OF CITY DWELLERS (1991)

89
57.6
U.K.

77
123.7
Japan

75
Total population (millions) 1,170.7
252.5
China
U.S.

33

THE WORLD'S 12 MAJOR LANGUAGES (1987)
(millions of speakers)

Mandarin Chinese and its dialects
Punjabi
English
Spanish
1,000
350
250
70
70
100
120
200
135
150
150
150
Russian
Hindi
Portuguese
Arabic
Japanese
Bengali
German
French
OTHER LANGUAGES 2.3 billion

◀ **The streets of Shanghai are some of the most crowded in China. Shanghai's population has increased from 5 million in 1948 to almost 8.3 million in 1993.**

◀ **There are posters throughout China encouraging couples to have only one child. China's population has grown from 540 million in 1949 to 1.2 billion in 1993.**

Half of the population in China is under 30 years of age, but living standards and medical conditions have improved over the last 40 years, and people are now living longer. About 80 percent of the people live in the east and southeast, on about a fifth of the total land. The government does not encourage people to move from the countryside to the cities, or from one city to another.

CITIES AND COUNTRYSIDE
About 33 percent of the people live in cities, towns, and rural townships (new developments in the countryside). The cities are mostly situated in the east of the country, and 40 of them have populations of over one million. They are all growing. The current figures for cities do not reflect the fact that many people from the countryside are moving there without government permission, in the hope of finding work. Towns are also growing, and the rural townships have developed since the late 1970s, because the government's economic changes have

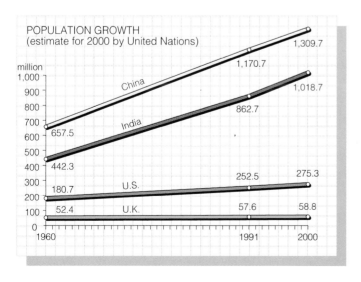

POPULATION GROWTH
(estimate for 2000 by United Nations)

million
1,000
900
800
700
600
500
400
300
200
100
0

China
1,309.7
1,170.7
657.5

India
1,018.7
862.7
442.3

U.S.
252.5
275.3
180.7

U.K.
52.4
57.6
58.8

1960
1991
2000

The Tibetan people live in the west of China. They are very religious and regard the Dalai Lama, who has lived in exile in India since 1959, as their leader.

allowed small industries in areas where most people used to work on the land.

About 67 percent of Chinese people live in the countryside. They are mainly farmers and peasants. As it is such a large country, their homes and life-styles vary. During the cold winters in northern China, peasants might sleep, eat, and sit on a *kang*. A *kang* is a platform of loose clay bricks, which is heated by the small wood-burning stove where they do their cooking. In contrast, in the warm southwest some country people live in straw houses built on stilts.

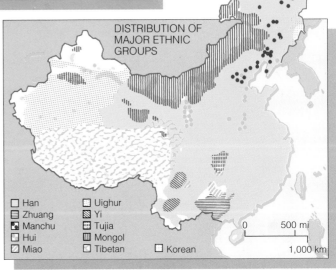

DISTRIBUTION OF MAJOR ETHNIC GROUPS

☐ Han
☐ Zhuang
☐ Manchu
☐ Hui
☐ Miao
☐ Uighur
☒ Yi
☐ Tujia
☐ Mongol
☐ Tibetan
☐ Korean

0   500 mi
1,000 km

LANGUAGE

The Chinese language is spoken in different dialects throughout the country, though the written forms are the same. The standard form of spoken Chinese is Mandarin, based on a northern dialect from the Beijing area. Cantonese is spoken in the area around Guangzhou.

THE MINORITY NATIONALITIES

Approximately 92 percent of the people in China are Han Chinese, whom we would regard as typical Chinese. The rest are of different ethnic origins, for example the Tibetans and the Koreans. There are 55 of these groups, totaling about 70 million people. The Chinese call these people

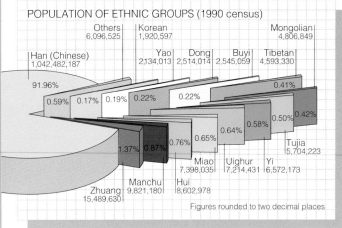

POPULATION OF ETHNIC GROUPS (1990 census)

Others 6,096,525	Korean 1,920,597					Mongolian 4,806,849
Han (Chinese) 1,042,482,187	Yao 2,134,013	Dong 2,514,014	Buyi 2,545,059	Tibetan 4,593,330		
91.96%						0.41%
0.59% 0.17% 0.19% 0.22%	0.22%				0.50% 0.42%	
		0.64%	0.58%			
1.37% 0.87% 0.76%	0.65%				Tujia 5,704,223	
	Miao 7,398,035	Uighur 7,214,431	Yi 6,572,173			
Zhuang 15,489,630	Manchu 9,821,180	Hui 8,602,978				

Figures rounded to two decimal places

◀ *The Uighurs are a Muslim people who live in the northwest of China in Xinjiang Autonomous Region. Their language is closely related to Turkish, and they write in Arabic script.*

◀ *Almost 2 million Bai people live in Yunnan province in southwest China. There are 21 other minority groups in this province.*

the minority nationalities. They usually have a different language, different customs, and a different religion than the Han Chinese. The minorities are scattered over 50 percent of the territory, though they tend to be concentrated in the border and mountain regions.

Some minorities, such as the Tibetans and the Uighurs, want independence. The government has encouraged the Han Chinese to move to minority regions, with the result that they now often outnumber the minority peoples in some of these areas. The one-child policy is not applied as strictly among the minority groups.

DAILY LIFE

Both urban and rural areas of China are changing and becoming more modern. Since the early 1980s, a growing number of Western goods and influences have been affecting people's lives. For example, in 1984 only 3 percent of Beijing households had refrigerators, but by 1989, the number had risen to 60 percent.

FAMILY LIFE

In the past most people in cities and towns were assigned to jobs for life. Housing accommodations usually came with the job. Things are beginning to change. Students and other people can apply for jobs, while in some cities and countryside areas people are now allowed to buy or build their own homes. Because there are housing shortages in the cities, many young people live with their parents. People tend to go shopping every day, even if they have refrigerators. Shopping is a social event.

Traditionally, the family plays a very

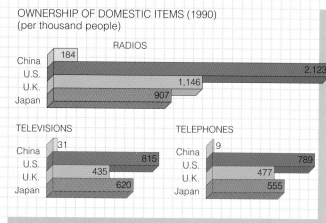

OWNERSHIP OF DOMESTIC ITEMS (1990)
(per thousand people)

RADIOS

China	184
U.S.	2,123
U.K.	1,146
Japan	907

TELEVISIONS

China	31
U.S.	815
U.K.	435
Japan	620

TELEPHONES

China	9
U.S.	789
U.K.	477
Japan	555

◀ *Most people in the cities live in small apartments. Their homes usually have no hot running water, and they often have to use communal showers. Sometimes people have to share cooking facilities.*

▶ *Teahouses are popular places for men to meet and chat.*

People often play board games on the street, with spectators watching and encouraging. Other games include cards and ping pong (played on a concrete table, using bricks for a net).

important part in Chinese life, and the Communist Party has reinforced this idea. Chinese people have a lot of respect for senior citizens.

EDUCATION

Education is supposed to be compulsory for nine years, but it is not available to all children in remote areas. In addition, farmers and peasants often take their children out of school early because they want them to help work on the land. Daughters are less likely to receive an education. About 22 percent of the population is illiterate or semiliterate, but this is a great improvement on the figure of 80 percent in 1949.

In the cities, many young children go to all-day kindergartens, so their mothers can work full-time. Otherwise, children start school at the age of six. They go to primary school for five or six years; junior middle school for three years; and senior middle school for two or three years. There are exams at the end of primary school and at the end of junior and senior middle school. There are also "key schools," which provide the best education for entry to universities. Parents in the cities are anxious to send their children to these schools. Only a small percentage of pupils go on to higher education.

The school day runs from 8 A.M. to noon and from 2 P.M. to 4 P.M. Pupils have homework as well. There are two terms in the year. The first lasts from September to January, with a month off for the Spring Festival holiday. The second is from February or March to June, with two months' summer vacation.

LEISURE

The Chinese work a six-day week (Monday to Saturday), but they do have a long lunch break, with a nap. Sunday is the day when

KEY FACTS

● The Chinese place the family name first. In the name Wu Xiaopei, the family name is Wu. Outside the family, people are usually called by the family name.
● The mother keeps her maiden name when she marries; a child takes the father's family name.
● The given name usually has a meaning. For instance, Xiaopei means Little Jewel.
● In 1982, 0.6% of the population graduated from higher education. In 1990 the figure was 1.4%.
● The legal age for men to marry is 22. For women it is 20.
● A factory often has its own health center and sometimes a small hospital, too.
● In 1989, China had 1,010 people per doctor, compared with 419 in the United States.

everyone in the cities goes to the parks.

Because living conditions are often cramped, people carry out their leisure activities outside the home. These vary from traditional Chinese activities to modern Western ones. In the early morning old people do T'AI CHI CH'UAN in the parks and as they wait for buses. In the evenings young people play pool on tables in the streets. Others gather to hear live traditional Chinese opera, or pop music on

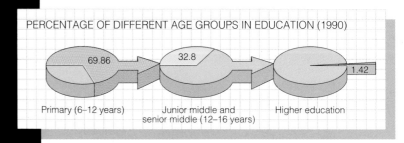

PERCENTAGE OF DIFFERENT AGE GROUPS IN EDUCATION (1990)

69.86   32.8   1.42

Primary (6–12 years)   Junior middle and senior middle (12–16 years)   Higher education

◀ *Physical exercise is an important part of the school curriculum. Pupils usually have to do 10 minutes of set exercises every morning before classes begin.*

▼ *A boy practices the traditional way to write Chinese characters with a brush and ink.*

a tape recorder, or to join ballroom dancing classes. In the countryside, traveling street theater, weight lifting, and open-air movies are popular. Men often gather in teahouses to drink tea, chat, and smoke. About 70 percent of Chinese men smoke, and this is a growing health problem.

Discos and *karaoke* are popular among young people. Eating with family and friends has always been a social pastime for all ages. The lottery has become very popular in Guangzhou. In the cities people keep birds and goldfish as pets. Goldfish are supposed to be lucky. The most popular sports are volleyball and table tennis.

RELIGION AND CULTURE

Officially religion is allowed in China, but it is not encouraged. Communists do not

一 YE (1)
二 ER (2)
三 SAN (3)
四 SI (4)
五 WU (5)
六 LIU (6)
七 QI (7)
八 BA (8)
九 JIU (9)
十 SHI (10)

明 YUE (moon)
月 RI (sun)
木 MU (tree or wood)
山 SHAN (mountain)
人 REN (man or person)
子 ZI (child or seed)
中国 ZHONGGUO (China)
ZHONG (middle) GUO (country)

◀ ▲ *The Chinese have no alphabet. They write using diagrams called characters. Words are made up of one or more characters. There are over 60,000 characters in the Chinese language. About 4,000 are needed for a basic level of literacy and to read a newspaper. Children have to learn 400–500 characters a year at school.*

approve of religion, and in the 1960s and 1970s many religious places in China were closed. The government has recently become more tolerant, and people are beginning to set up family shrines again, where they can worship their ancestors. Many temples, mosques, and churches have reopened.

The main religion in China is Buddhism. Daoism and ancestor worship are other traditional beliefs. There are also temples dedicated to Confucius, a Chinese scholar and philosopher who lived 2,500 years ago. He drew up strict rules for life that included respecting senior citizens. Islam, Christianity, and Judaism are also practiced in China.

Both modern Western medical techniques and traditional Chinese medicine are used in China. In Chinese medicine the belief is that the whole body should be balanced if it is to work properly. Medicines are made from a mixture of herbs. In acupuncture, needles

▼ *Spectators watch a Dragon Dance during the Spring Festival, the Chinese New Year. This is the main holiday of the year, and many people travel long distances to be with their families.*

FESTIVALS AND HOLIDAYS

January 1	NEW YEAR Public holiday
Jan./Feb. (movable)	SPRING FESTIVAL (CHINESE NEW YEAR) 3-day public holiday
April 5	QING MING Remembering the dead
May 1	WORKERS' DAY Public holiday. People have free entry to parks.
May/June (movable)	DRAGON BOAT FESTIVAL
June 1	CHILDREN'S DAY
August 1	ARMY DAY To show respect for the army
Sept./Oct. (movable)	MOON FESTIVAL Like a harvest festival; held at the full moon. "Mooncakes" are eaten.
October 1	NATIONAL DAY 2-day public holiday. Celebrates the day when Mao Zedong proclaimed the People's Republic in 1949.

KEY FACTS

● The Chinese drink tea with no milk or sugar.
● Throughout China, people keep boiled water in thermoses for drinking, because tap water is not safe to drink.

◀ *Two men practice t'ai chi ch'uan outside the walls of the Forbidden City, the old imperial palace in the center of Beijing.*

▼ *Visitors to Sanyuangong shrine in Guangdong province. After a period of repression, religion in China is now on the increase again.*

▶ *The different regions of China have their own traditional styles of opera. The stories are based on old legends and events in history. The makeup and clothes of a theatrical character are very important. A red beard in Beijing Opera, for example, means courage. The actors paint their own faces, and this can sometimes take up to 3 hours. The flags on the back of this character from Beijing Opera show that he is a general.*

are applied to specific points on the body to help ease and cure ailments. Qi Gong is a way of creating high energy through meditation, while t'ai chi ch'uan and martial arts are also based on meditation principles.

SOCIAL PROBLEMS

The economic changes in China have affected people's lives. A large gap is developing between the incomes of those working in the state sector, like teachers and state factory employees, and the owners of new businesses. Inflation is high. The crime rate has been low for many years, but it is now growing. Women have been officially equal in law since 1949, but in practice they still do most of the housework and have less important jobs. Divorce is difficult to obtain, but the rates are beginning to rise.

The National People's Congress meets in the Great Hall of the People in Tiananmen Square in Beijing, which was built in 10 months from 1958–1959. It is opposite the old palace of the Chinese emperors.

In 1911 the last Chinese emperor was deposed, and a republic was established. After a period of civil war and changing governments, the Nationalist Party was defeated by the Communists, who formed the People's Republic of China in 1949, headed by Chairman Mao Zedong. The Chinese Communist Party (CCP) has ruled China ever since, except for the island of Taiwan (which used to be governed from the mainland), where the Nationalists set up the Republic of China (ROC).

There are various governing bodies in the People's Republic of China, at both national and local levels. They all exist alongside the CCP structure. The National People's Congress (NPC) is the central parliament, and it meets for two or three weeks once a year. Representatives are elected every five years by the local congresses all over China, which represent the 22 provinces, 5 autonomous regions,

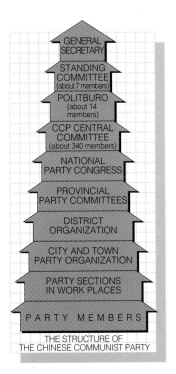

THE STRUCTURE OF THE CHINESE COMMUNIST PARTY

- GENERAL SECRETARY
- STANDING COMMITTEE (about 7 members)
- POLITBURO (about 14 members)
- CCP CENTRAL COMMITTEE (about 340 members)
- NATIONAL PARTY CONGRESS
- PROVINCIAL PARTY COMMITTEES
- DISTRICT ORGANIZATION
- CITY AND TOWN PARTY ORGANIZATION
- PARTY SECTIONS IN WORK PLACES
- PARTY MEMBERS

Members of the Chinese Communist Party (CCP), China's most important governing body, are active at every level of society.

Most of the representatives in the National People's Congress are also Communist Party members.

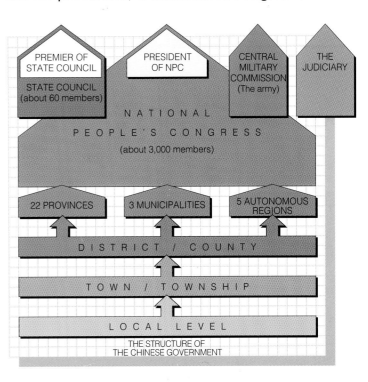

THE STRUCTURE OF THE CHINESE GOVERNMENT

- PREMIER OF STATE COUNCIL — STATE COUNCIL (about 60 members)
- PRESIDENT OF NPC
- CENTRAL MILITARY COMMISSION (The army)
- THE JUDICIARY

NATIONAL PEOPLE'S CONGRESS (about 3,000 members)

- 22 PROVINCES
- 3 MUNICIPALITIES
- 5 AUTONOMOUS REGIONS

DISTRICT / COUNTY

TOWN / TOWNSHIP

LOCAL LEVEL

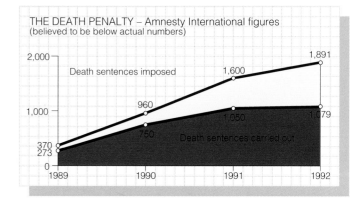

In 1989 people filled Tiananmen Square for several weeks in peaceful demonstrations to demand political reforms. On June 4 the government sent in soldiers and tanks against them. Many were killed.

The death penalty exists for various crimes, including murder, rape, and some political offenses.

and 3 municipalities. The autonomous regions are areas where large groupings of minority people live, for example Ningxia and Guizhou.

The NPC discusses and approves plans for the national economy and decides whether to go to war. It selects the main officials and groups to run the country. The country is controlled by these and by other influential people, who are often retired from all official posts, such as Deng Xiaoping, former chairman of the Communist Party and former chairman of the Central Military Commission (the army).

The top government posts are all held by members of the CCP. The Standing Committee and Politburo of the CCP are the most powerful bodies in the country and deal with all major issues. Senior army personnel are also often appointed to government positions.

The CCP has to approve all election candidates. Many of the positions in government are filled by people who are

THE DEATH PENALTY – Amnesty International figures
(believed to be below actual numbers)

Death sentences imposed

Death sentences carried out

	1989	1990	1991	1992
Death sentences imposed	370	960	1,600	1,891
Death sentences carried out	273	750	1,050	1,079

appointed to the posts rather than being elected. This system sometimes causes dissatisfaction, with people demanding freer elections and more choice over who governs the country. This was one of the main causes of the protests in Tiananmen Square in the spring of 1989, which led to the government sending in troops against the protesters.

People who have disagreed with the system in China are often sent to remote labor camps. This system is known as "reform through labor."

ARTICLE 1 OF THE CONSTITUTION OF THE PEOPLE'S REPUBLIC OF CHINA:

"The People's Republic of China is a socialist state under the people's democratic dictatorship led by the working class and based on the alliance of workers and peasants.

The socialist system is the basic system of the People's Republic of China. Disruption of the socialist system by any organization or individual is prohibited."

▼*National Day parade in Beijing. China's army is called the People's Liberation Army (PLA). It has about 3 million members.*

KEY FACTS

● Beijing means "northern capital." *Bei* means "north", *jing* means "capital."
● Nanjing, which was a capital city in the past, means "southern capital."
● Article 48 of the Constitution states that women are equal with men in all spheres of life.
● In 1993 the most senior woman in the Chinese government was the minister of foreign trade, Mrs. Wu Yi.
● There are 1,936 counties in China.
● Many people on the police force are armed with electric batons.
● The number of crimes being committed by young people is increasing.

FOOD AND FARMING

Rice is the staple food for most people in China, especially in the south. In the north and west it is too dry to grow rice, so people there also use wheat flour to make noodles and bread. All grain crops are rationed and heavily subsidized. Meat is only eaten a couple of times a week, usually pork (except for the Muslims) or chicken. People eat mutton more in western China, where they graze sheep on the hills.

▼ *Most farmers in China use traditional methods to plant and tend their crops. They push tractors by hand and use oxen to pull plows.*

The Chinese eat fish from both rivers and the ocean, and there are fish farms in the east. Since China covers such a large area, there is a great diversity of fruit and vegetables, ranging from melons to apples and from Chinese cabbages to peppers.

Traditionally, the Han Chinese do not eat much dairy produce. In the past they used all the available land for growing crops. Now imports of grain are increasing to feed the growing number of dairy animals that are being kept.

Chinese cooking is famous the world over, and there are many regional variations in dishes. In the north of China, *jiaozi*, or

KEY FACTS

● China is feeding more than a fifth of the world's population on 7 percent of the world's arable land.

● China is the world's biggest producer of wheat.

● Rice has been cultivated in China for over 5,000 years.

● In 1990, China produced and consumed almost 191 million tons of rice — nearly 16 times the amount that was traded on the entire world market.

● Soup is usually served at the end of a meal in China.

dumplings, are made by family and friends for the Spring Festival and other gatherings. In the south tiny flavored snacks, called dim sum, are popular. Sichuan and Hunan provinces are famous for hot, spicy food. Mealtimes are a very important part of family life. Families get together, and adults and children even travel home for lunch from work and school, if they can.

China is still mainly an agricultural country, although only 11 percent of the land is suitable for growing crops. The most intensively farmed land is in the east and the center. Some land is very productive,

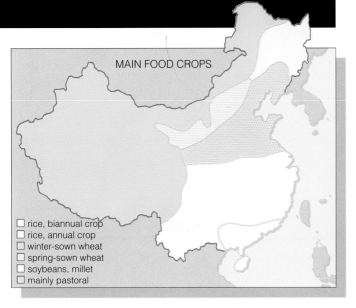

MAIN FOOD CROPS

☐ rice, biannual crop
☐ rice, annual crop
☐ winter-sown wheat
☐ spring-sown wheat
☐ soybeans, millet
☐ mainly pastoral

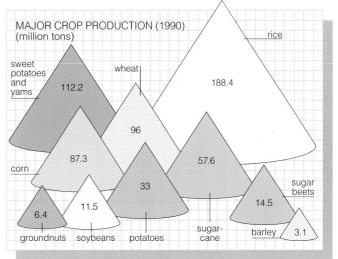

MAJOR CROP PRODUCTION (1990)
(million tons)

rice 188.4

sweet potatoes and yams 112.2

wheat 96

corn 87.3

potatoes 33

sugar-cane 57.6

soybeans 11.5

groundnuts 6.4

sugar beets 14.5

barley 3.1

► **Planting a rice paddy field in Guilin, south China. In some areas farmers can harvest a rice crop two or three times a year.**

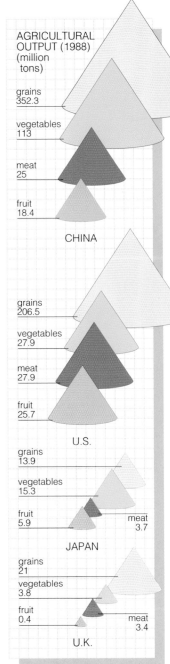

◀ Many shops in China still use abacuses to calculate the cost of purchases.

▼ To prepare a traditional meal, the food is cut into small pieces and cooked in a WOK. The different dishes are placed on the table for all to share.

AGRICULTURAL OUTPUT (1988) (million tons)

CHINA
grains 352.3
vegetables 113
meat 25
fruit 18.4

U.S.
grains 206.5
vegetables 27.9
meat 27.9
fruit 25.7

JAPAN
grains 13.9
vegetables 15.3
fruit 5.9
meat 3.7

U.K.
grains 21
vegetables 3.8
fruit 0.4
meat 3.4

such as the Sichuan Basin, and can produce two or three harvests a year. At present China can just about manage to feed all its people, but the continually increasing population means it might not be able to do so for much longer. Most farming is still done in the traditional way. Besides rice and wheat, agricultural products include soybeans, barley, sorghum, oats, potatoes, tea, oilseed crops, and sugarcane. Cotton and rubber are important industrial crops.

Between 1958 and 1978, all food in China was grown by COMMUNES and had to be sold to the government at a fixed price. Since 1978, individual farmers and peasants have been allowed to rent land. After selling a certain amount of produce at a set price to the government, they can take the rest to the new free markets. There they can sell it for whatever price people are prepared to pay. Some farmers have made a lot of money over the last few years. They are building new houses for themselves, which are using up valuable farmland.

TRADE AND INDUSTRY

China's industries are mainly situated in the east and central parts of the country. Many of the northern industrial cities are near sites of coal and iron ore. When the Communists came to power in 1949, one of their main goals was to speed up industrialization. They favored heavy industries, such as steelworks. In the 1980s, China produced about 50 million tons of pig iron and 56 million tons of crude steel annually. Today, while these industries are still important, there is a shift to light industries, such as the production of consumer goods (refrigerators, TVs, etc.), and to service industries, such as banking and insurance.

This reflects the enormous changes currently taking place in China's trade and industry. Until recently all places of work, known as "work units," were run by the state and controlled by the Communist Party. Since the early 1980s, the government has freed some companies and factories from state control and allowed private individuals to set up businesses. Foreigners are now allowed to invest in China.

SPECIAL ECONOMIC ZONES

In 1980 the government declared four Special Economic Zones (SEZs) along the coast, in Shenzhen, Zhuhai, Shantou, and Xiamen. Hainan Island was added in 1988. These are areas where Chinese people and foreigners are encouraged to invest and start businesses without some of the

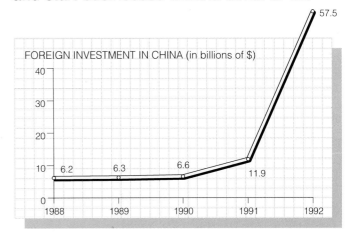

FOREIGN INVESTMENT IN CHINA (in billions of $)

57.5
6.2   6.3   6.6   11.9
1988   1989   1990   1991   1992

▶*Shanghai's stock exchange opened in 1990 as part of the government's economic development policies. A second stock exchange opened in Shenzhen in 1991.*

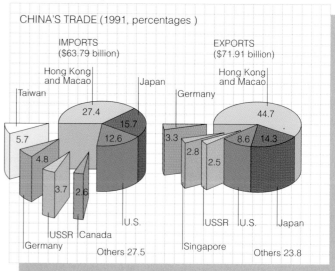

CHINA'S TRADE (1991, percentages)

IMPORTS
($63.79 billion)

Hong Kong
and Macao

Taiwan

Japan

27.4

15.7

5.7

12.6

4.8

3.7 2.6

U.S.

USSR Canada

Germany

Others 27.5

EXPORTS
($71.91 billion)

Hong Kong
and Macao

Germany

44.7

3.3

8.6 14.3

2.8

2.5

USSR U.S. Japan

Singapore

Others 23.8

▲*Chinese factories are now producing consumer goods, such as televisions, after years of concentrating on heavy industry.*

restrictions imposed by the Communist system in the rest of China. Guangdong province, where two of these zones are situated, is the fastest developing area in Asia. Foreign companies can now invest in other coastal areas and in inland regions as well. Many of these foreign companies work jointly with Chinese companies.

IMPORTS AND EXPORTS

Some of China's most important exports are clothing, cotton yarn, woven fabrics, machinery, electronic products, crude petroleum, and refined petroleum products. China is now a major center for assembling parts for computers and other industries. All these goods bring foreign currency into the country, which China can use to buy equipment for its modernization program. Major imports in 1990 included materials and parts for processing, machinery and electronic products, steel products, and fertilizers.

★SPECIAL ECONOMIC
ZONES

FUJIAN

GUANGDONG

Xiamen ★

★ Shantou

Zhuhai★ ★Shenzhen

MACAO HONG KONG

★ Hainan

▲*Shenzhen is one of China's Special Economic Zones (SEZs), where incentives such as low taxes encourage Chinese and foreigners to develop businesses.*

THE GROWTH
OF CHINA'S
TRADE

billions $

84.99 (1992)
80.60 (1992)
71.91 (1991)
63.79 (1991)
62.09
53.34
42.25
27.35
19.55
18.27
7.49
7.26
2.33
2.26

IMPORTS
EXPORTS

60 —
50 —
40 —
30 —
20 —
10 —
0 —

1970   1975   1980   1985   1990   1995

KEY FACTS

● In all but three provinces, municipalities, or autonomous regions, industry accounts for at least a third of the local income.

● In 1991, the Chinese provinces with the highest industrial output were Jiangsu (Y 256,393 million), Guangdong (Y 204,556 million), and Shandong (Y 185,692 million).

● Toys, games, and sporting goods accounted for 14.4 percent of the American imports from China in 1992. Clothing accounted for 17.4 percent and footwear for 13.2 percent.

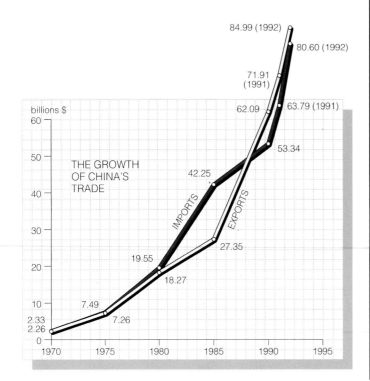

◀ *Tourism is developing in China. The Great Wall is one of the most famous sites from the country's long history that all visitors want to see. It was originally begun by the first emperor over 2,000 years ago, when he linked up the existing walls of different kingdoms to prevent invasions from the north.*

EFFECTS OF THE NEW POLICIES

Besides these changes in large industries, the new government policies have made it possible for individuals or small businesses to make a great deal of money from activities such as selling goods in the free markets. They deal in everything from bananas to motorcycles and from kitchen utensils to underwear.

Some people say that the new government policies mean China is becoming more like a capitalist country and that it can no longer call itself a Communist country. Deng Xiaoping, who was a leading force behind the push for economic reforms, has said, "It doesn't matter what color the cat is, black or white, as long as it catches the mouse."

TRANSPORTATION

Despite its size and difficult terrain, public transportation in China is fairly good. Most people travel long distances by train rather than bus or airplane, because the roads are poor and flying is expensive.

There is a railroad network to all of the provinces except Tibet, although one is now being constructed. Special railroads serve factories and mines. It takes 33 hours to travel the 1,434 miles (2,313 km) from

▲ *The bicycle is the main form of private transportation in China*

◄ *Sixty people can sleep in a train's "hard sleeper" carriage. The bunks are in groups of six and open out onto the corridor. During the day, people sit on the bottom bunks, play cards, and talk.*

KEY FACTS

● During the wet season, the Yangtze River, one of China's main transportation systems, is navigable by 15,000 ton ships as far as Wuhan, more than 928 miles (1,000 km) inland.
● In 1990, 47 Chinese airports were able to handle Boeing 737s and larger aircraft.
● Chinese airlines carried a total of 16,596,000 passengers in 1990.
● In 1990, the total length of the railroad network was 32,635 miles (53,378 km).

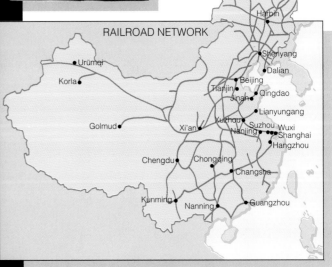

RAILROAD NETWORK

Harbin
Ürümqi
Korla
Shenyang
Dalian
Beijing
Tianjin
Jinan
Qingdao
Lianyungang
Golmud
Xi'an
Xuzhou
Suzhou
Wuxi
Nanjing
Shanghai
Hangzhou
Chengdu
Chongqing
Changsha
Kunming
Nanning
Guangzhou

NUMBER OF BICYCLES AND CARS (millions, mid-1980s)

	Bicycles	Cars
China	300	1.2
India	45	1.5
Mexico	12	4.8
Netherlands	11	4.9
Japan	60	30.7
West Germany	45	26
U.S.	103	139

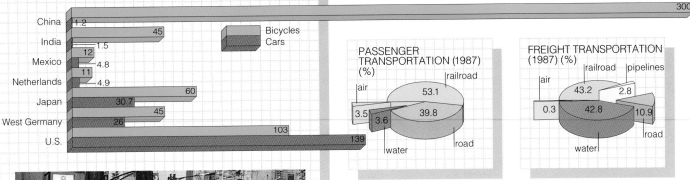

PASSENGER TRANSPORTATION (1987) (%)

air 3.5
water 3.6
road 39.8
railroad 53.1

FREIGHT TRANSPORTATION (1987) (%)

air 0.3
water 42.8
road 10.9
railroad 43.2
pipelines 2.8

Beijing to Guangzhou by train. The average train ride in China lasts 10 hours. More than 70 percent of towns and villages are connected to the main road system. Rivers and canals are used to take passengers and freight inland.

In the cities the buses are cheap and plentiful but always overcrowded. Beijing and Tianjin both have subway systems, built in the early 1980s.

◀ *Road congestion is becoming serious in some cities. There are few privately owned cars, but the number is growing, with sales up by 40 percent in 1992.*

▶ *The CAAC (Civil Aviation Administration of China) licenses and operates China's airlines. Air traffic is growing by 30 percent a year.*

THE ENVIRONMENT

The pulp and paper industry causes a sixth of the water pollution in China. This could rapidly increase, as currently the amount of paper used per person in the country is very low. The tanning industry is another serious source of water pollution.

China already has environmental problems, which seem likely to worsen as the country modernizes and becomes richer. Currently in China an average of 1 ton of coal is used per person per year, ten times less than the figure in the United States. If China starts to use the same amount of coal as the West does, this will have serious effects on global warming.

Industry is responsible for about 70 percent of the pollution in China. Many industrial cities suffer from acid rain, and most rivers passing through major cities are severely polluted. Chinese industries often use large amounts of raw materials, including water and energy, in relation to their output.

In an attempt to get as much produce as possible from the small amount of crop-growing land, some areas have been farmed too intensively, and often pesticides and fertilizers have been overused. In addition, the growing population in the cities is forcing developments to be built on valuable farmland.

On the northern grasslands of China the desert is expanding, because over-grazing has left too little grass to hold the soil in place. Cutting down too many trees has meant that the forests in western Sichuan, where the giant pandas live, are getting smaller, despite the creation of several nature reserves. Other animals, such as bears and tigers, are under threat because of their use in traditional Chinese medicine.

The government is aware of the problems and has set up the Natural Environmental Protection Agency (NEPA) to try and do something about them. One project it has organized is a massive tree-planting campaign, known as "The Green Wall" campaign, to try and prevent farmland in northern China from being washed or blown away. The government is also trying to reduce pollution from some industries, such as coal and oil producers and manufacturers of chemicals, metals, food, and building materials.

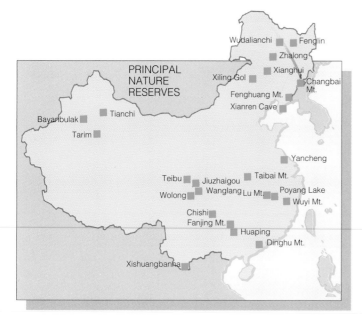

PRINCIPAL NATURE RESERVES

Wudalianchi Fenglin
Zhalong
Xianghui
Xiling Gol
Fenghuang Mt.
Changbai Mt.
Xianren Cave
Bayanbulak Tianchi
Tarim
Yancheng
Teibu Taibai Mt.
Jiuzhaigou
Wolong Wanglang Lu Mt. Poyang Lake
Chishi Wuyi Mt.
Fanjing Mt.
Huaping
Dinghu Mt.
Xishuangbanna

◀ **There are over 350 nature reserves in China.**

▼ **The giant panda is the symbol of the World Wide Fund for Nature. It only lives in the forests of western Sichuan province and eats a specific type of bamboo shoot that grows there. Because these forests are being cut down, there are now only 700 giant pandas left in the wild.**

KEY FACTS

● In one single reserve in Sichuan province there are 4,000 species of native plants — more than in all of Europe.

● In many cities coal briquettes are burned for fuel, which means coal dust adds to the pollution.

● Yunnan province has over 2,000 plant species that can be used in medicines.

● Many village communities dump their plant, animal, and human waste, together with water, into airtight concrete containers. The mixture ferments and produces methane gas, which is used for fuel.

THE FUTURE

The People's Republic of China is changing very fast. The new economic reforms are bringing prosperity to some people but not to others, and this is causing resentment. The challenge for the Chinese government now is to develop the economy without causing too many problems in society.

Currently China is one country. However, many factors could lead to it breaking up into different states. Economic developments are increasing the differences between the underdeveloped states and those that are more advanced. In addition, the Tibetans in the west would like to break away to form their own country, while the Uighurs in the northwest are also starting to call for greater independence.

One of China's major problems is the steady growth of its population, which brings heavy demands on the nation's resources. The government is trying to limit population growth, but the real effects of the one-child policy will not begin to be seen until the next century. The Chinese are also concerned that all these single children will be spoiled by their families. Also, as technology increases, there will inevitably be growing unemployment in the countryside.

It is always possible that China might once again close its doors on the outside world. Until the 1980s, very few foreigners were allowed into the country, but now many work and travel there. Throughout history, China has always wanted Western technology but not Western culture. However, it is more likely that China will keep in contact with other countries and perhaps become one of the most powerful countries in the world. The Chinese people are used to being patient and looking ahead to the future. A Chinese saying states: "You have to water the seed to see the tree."

◄Over the last 10 years, Western influences have affected all aspects of life in China. A trip to the new McDonald's in Beijing is now part of the sight-seeing trip for a family visiting from the countryside.

▼Hong Kong, a small island off the southern coast of China, has been ruled by Great Britain since 1841. It is now a major capitalist economy, and, under the terms of a treaty between Great Britain and China signed in 1898, Hong Kong is due to be returned to mainland China in 1997. Deng Xiaoping has said that, although Hong Kong will be part of Communist China, it will remain a financial center: "One country, two systems."

KEY FACTS

● China is a nuclear power and has been testing weapons in the Taklimakan Desert.
● China has been launching satellites into space since 1970.
● During the 1990s, the Chinese population will increase by about 125 million people — equivalent to half the population of the United States.
● By the year 2035, more than a quarter of China's population will be over 65 years old.
● The island of Macao is being returned to China by Portugal in 1999.
● Mainland China would also like to regain control over Taiwan, which is currently an independent republic.

FURTHER INFORMATION

- CENTER FOR TEACHING ABOUT CHINA
1201 W. Schwartz, Carbondale, IL 62901
- CHINA INSTITUTE IN AMERICA
125 E. 65th Street, New York, NY 10021
- CHINA NATIONAL TOURIST OFFICE
333 W. Broadway, Suite 201,
Glendale, CA 91204
- CHINESE TOURIST BOARD
60 E. 42nd Street, New York, NY 10165
- CONSULATE OF THE PEOPLE'S REPUBLIC OF CHINA
520 12th Avenue, New York, NY 10036
- U.S–CHINA PEOPLE'S FRIENDSHIP ASSOCIATION
2025 Eye Street N.W. #715,
Washington, D.C. 20016

BOOKS ABOUT CHINA

Merton, D. and Yun-Kan, Shio. *China: The Land & Its People*, Silver Burdett, 1991

Odijk, Pamela. *The Chinese.* Silver Burdett, 1991

Steele, Philip. *China.* Raintree Steck-Vaughn, 1990

Stewart, Gail B. *China.* Macmillan Child Group, 1990

ROMANIZATION

In this book Chinese characters are romanized (written in the alphabet used by Western countries) according to the form called pinyin, which is used by the PRC. The standard romanization used in Hong Kong and Taiwan is different.

PINYIN	TRADITIONAL
Beijing	Peking
Guangzhou	Canton
Mao Zedong	Mao Tse-tung
Zhongguo (China)	Chung-kuo
Xinjiang	Sinkiang
Sichuan	Szechwan
Daoism	Taoism

GLOSSARY

BUDDHISM
A religion that originated in India in the 5th century B.C. and came to China in the 1st century A.D.

CAPITALISM
An economic system in which individuals own businesses and keep the profits

COMMUNE
A group of villages where the peasants share and work the land together. All produce has to be sold to the government at a set price.

COMMUNISM
An economic and political system in which private ownership is abolished, and all industry is controlled by the state

DAOISM
A Chinese religion and philosophy that teaches that people should live in harmony with nature

FREE MARKET
A market where goods can be bought and sold at whatever price people are prepared to pay, often with some haggling

LOESS
The accumulation of fine, light-colored grains of clay or silt deposited by the wind

T'AI CHI CH'UAN
A form of exercise and meditation

WOK
A large metal pan, used to stir-fry food in Chinese cooking

INDEX

© Simon and Schuster
Young Books 1994

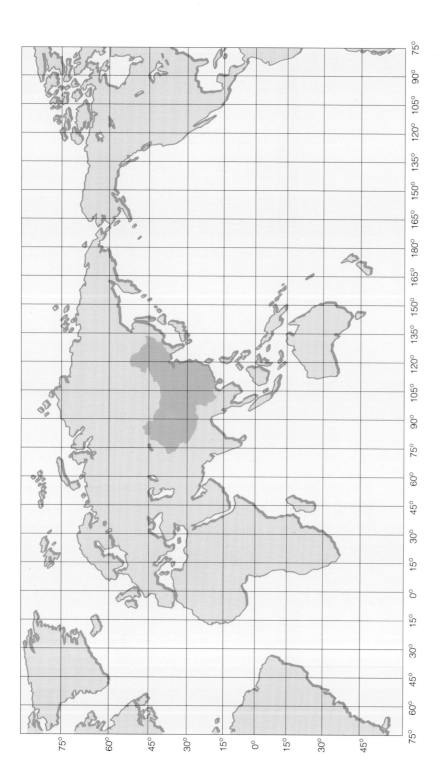

In addition to China's 22 provinces, there are:

5 AUTONOMOUS REGIONS

NEI MONGGOL (Inner Mongolia)
XIZANG (Tibet)
XINJIANG UYGUR
GUANGXI
NINGXIA

3 MUNICIPALITIES

BEIJING
TIANJIN
SHANGHAI

DATE DUE
